The Eighteenth Century in English Caricature

SELWYN BRINTON

1904

TABLE OF CONTENTS

INTRODUCTORY

The word Caricature does not lend itself easily to precise definition. Etymologically it connects itself with the Italian caricare, to load or charge, thus corresponding precisely in derivation with its French equivalent Charge; and—save a yet earlier reference in Sir Thomas Browne—it first appears, as far as I am aware, in that phrase of No. 537 of the Spectator, "Those burlesque pictures which the Italians call caracaturas."

Putting the dry bones of etymology from our thought the essence, the life-blood of the thing itself, is surely this—the human creature's amusement with itself and its environment, and its expression of that amusement through the medium of the plastic arts. So that our caracatura, our burlesque picture of life, stands on the same basis as comedy or satire, is, in fact, but comedy or satire finding its outlet in another form of expression. And this is so true that wherever we find brilliant or trenchant satire of life there we may be sure, too, that caricature is not far absent. Pauson's grotesques are the correlative of the Comedies of Aristophanes; and when the development of both is not correlative, not simultaneous, it is surely because one or other has been checked by political or social conditions, which have been inherently antagonistic to its growth.

Those conditions—favourable or antagonistic—it becomes part of our inquiry at this point to examine. We have this to ask, even granting that our "burlesque picture" is a natural, almost a necessary, accompaniment of human life,—was found, we may quite safely assume, in the cave-dwelling of primitive man, who probably satirised with a flint upon its walls those troublesome neighbours of his, the mammoth and the megatherium,—peers out upon us from the complex culture of the Roman world in the clumsy graffito of the Crucifixion,—emerges in the Middle Ages in a turbulent growth of grotesque, wherein those grim figures of Death or Devil move through a maze of imagery often quaint and fantastic, sometimes obscene or terrible—takes a fresh start in the Passionals of Lucas Cranach, and can be traced in England through her Rebellion and Restoration up to the very confines of the eighteenth century. Why, we have to ask, even granting that William Hogarth's "monster Caricatura" is thus omnivorous and omnipresent, does he tower aloft in some countries and under some conditions to the majesty of a new art, and in others dwindle down to puny ridicule?

Taking the special subject of this little volume, the eighteenth century itself, we find little to interest us in French pictorial satire until that monstrous growth of political caricature created by the Revolution. Italy in the same period has but little to offer us, Germany as little or less; and it is to England that we must turn for the pictorial humour, whether social or political, of that interesting epoch. And this because the England of that time is a self-conscious creature, emergent from a successful struggle for freedom, and strong enough to enjoy a hearty laugh—even at her own expense. While the Bastille still frowns over France, the Inquisition and the Jesuits are an incubus upon Spain and Italy, while Germany is split up into little principalities, Dukedoms, Bishoprics, Palatinates, England has already won for herself the great boon of freedom of thought, freedom of speech, freedom of religious and political opinion. The satirist could here find expression and appreciation. The birth of the pictorial satirist who is the subject of my first chapter coincides pretty closely with the creation of that Tale of a Tub, of which Dean Swift, in all the ripeness of his later talent, exclaimed: "Good God! what genius I had when I wrote that book"; and no print from the artist's graver—even his "Stages of Cruelty," or his "Players dressing in a Barn"—could excel in coarseness of fibre the great satirist's Strephon and Chloe.

The pen of Swift and the graver of Hogarth in the early eighteenth century found in England conditions not very dissimilar to those which awaited Philipon and Honoré Daumier[1] in Paris of the early nineteenth century— that is, a public which had come through a period of intensely active political existence to a complete and complex self-consciousness, and which enjoyed (just as in Paris La Caricature, when suppressed, found a speedy successor in Le Charivari) sufficient political freedom to render criticism a possibility. And from Hogarth through Sandby and Sayer and Woodward to Henry William Bunbury, and onwards to that giant of political satire, James Gillray, and his vigorous contemporary Thomas Rowlandson, what a feast of material is spread before us; what an insight we may gain, not only into costume, manners, social life, but into the detailed political development of a fertile and fascinating period of history. In the earlier age Hogarth is ready to present the very London of his time in the levée and drawing-room, in the vice and extravagance of the rich, in the industrious and thriving citizen, and those lowest haunts where crime hoped to lurk undisturbed. In the century's close Gillray's pencil notes every change of the political kaleidoscope. In his prints we seem almost to hear the muffled roar of the Parisian mob, clamorous for more blood in those days of Terror; or we watch the giant forms of Pitt and Buonaparte fronting each other as the strife comes nearer home to Britain.

To attempt within the limits of this little volume to exhaust a subject so rich in magnificent material would be obviously impossible. All that is permitted me here by imperative limits of space is a sketch, where my matter tempts me sorely to a comprehensive study. Yet even the sketch may claim for itself a place beside the finished work of art, if—while omitting the detail which it was unable to include—it has yet secured for us the main outlines, the swing of the figure, the balance of light and shadow, the sweep and spacing of the horizon; just as the massed clouds in a Constable study can give us as keen artistic pleasure as the "Valley Farm," or his "Salisbury Cathedral." And thus I have attempted here not so much the history of the men, the catalogue of their achieved work—interesting or valuable though such a history or catalogue might be—as to show the spirit of the age itself reflected most faithfully, even when it seems most caricatured or burlesqued, by their brush or graver or pencil; to watch the grotesque visage and ignoble form of Vice traced by Hogarth's genius from the homes of London's luxury to her dens of hidden crime; to study the more refined, if somewhat weaker, social satire of Henry William Bunbury; to admire those magnificent political cartoons of James Gillray—colossal and overwhelming, even in their brutality or obscenity; and finally, to lose ourselves in the luxuriant and living growth of Thomas Rowlandson's pencil, recreating for us the features of an age that was, like himself, vigorous, buoyant, and expansive,—that true Age of Caricature, which is also known as the Eighteenth Century.

THE COMEDY OF VICE

The eighteenth century, which was to witness the magnificent and, in its own way, unequalled achievement of English art in the paintings of Reynolds, Romney, Gainsborough, Hoppner; in the engravings of Bartolozzi, Dalton, John Raphael Smith, and William Henry Ryland; in the caricatures, which we have just noted, of Bunbury, Rowlandson, and Gillray, was to open, not inappropriately, with the appearance and speedy recognition of a very individual and very characteristic genius—with the pictured comedies of William Hogarth.

A first survey of my subject led me for a moment to doubt how far my title would cover the creations of that incomparable humourist. He is, indeed, more than caricaturist in the sense in which we shall use this term of his artistic successors. His pictured moralities teem with portraits drawn from the very life. He is a satirist, as mordant and merciless as Juvenal, or, in his own day, the terrible Dean of St. Patrick's; from his house in Leicester Fields he looks out upon the London of his day, and probes with his remorseless brush or graver to the hidden roots of its follies, its vices, and crimes. "He may be said to have created," says one of his early biographers,[2] "a new species of painting, which may be termed the moral comic;" meaning, thereby, that the instinctive humour of the man's art is generally (not, as we shall see, always) directed to some moral purpose, some lesson of conduct to be thence derived. That is just where Hogarth connects himself, inevitably and intimately, with the Puritan England which had preceded him. Not for nothing had that century, into whose last years he was born, seen the great uprising of Puritan England,—the struggle for civil and political liberty, and its achievement,—the Ironsides of Cromwell with Bible and uplifted sword. That intensity of moral and spiritual conviction, that earnestness about life and its issues was yet in the nation's blood, and must find some outlet in the returning world of art, which its own austerity had banished; but, in another sense, mark how truly Hogarth connects himself with the later caricaturists of the coming age.

Beauty does not enter into his art,—most of all in that highest sense of plastic beauty of form, which the great Italians had so intensely felt, which the great English school, uprising in his own day, was in some measure to recover. At most a comely buxom wench steals sometimes slyly into his canvas or copper-plate—the two servant-maids in his print of "Morning" at Covent Garden, whom the roysterers turning out from Tom King's coffee-house are kissing in the Piazza; the demure and pretty Miss West, looking over a joint hymn book with the amorous—but industrious—apprentice; or that coy minx—most delicious of them all—who has just dozed off amid "The Sleeping Congregation," with her prayer-book opened at the fascinating page of Matrimony, and to whose luxuriant charms of face and form the eyes of the fat old clerk are stealthily directed. To Hogarth these are the incidents, not the inspiration, of his art. Lavater, that keen observer, aimed near to the mark when he wrote: "Il ne faut pas attendre beaucoup de noblesse de Hogarth. Le vrai beau n'étoit guère à la portée de ce peintre." It is, indeed, one of the unconscious ironies of art history that the artist, whose work shows least of its influence or attraction, should have devoted the one offspring of his pen to an Analysis of Beauty.

But it is when we turn to the humour of life, even in its most sordid tragedies, that his real strength appears. "Quelle richesse inexprimable"— says Lavater again, and no less justly—"dans les scènes comiques ou morales de la vie." None like Hogarth has characterised "the lowest types of modern humanity, has better depicted the drunken habits of the dregs of the people, the follies of life, and the horrors of vice." And it is just here, as I have hinted, that Hogarth connects himself with the later caricaturists.

It were quite possible to treat a purely moral story, such as that of "The Industrious and the Idle Apprentice," in a purely moral sentiment; but this is just what our artist cannot bring himself to do. He must have that touch of nature, and of humour, which makes the whole world kin. He must introduce the quarrelling cat and dog into the office scene between West and Goodchild, or the feline visitant whose apparition through the chimney disturbs Thomas Idle's unhallowed slumbers; he must accentuate the gormandising guests in the Sheriff's banquet, and the humours of the crowd even in a Tyburn execution. And in other subjects—where the moral lesson is either absent or less intrusive—the man's fancy runs absolutely riot in humorous observation. "The Distressed Poet," with the baby squalling in his bed, the poor wife stitching at his solitary pair of breeches, and a strapping milkmaid clamouring for payment of her account; "The Enraged Musician," with every conceivable pandemonium of noise congregated beneath his window; above all, "The Sleeping Congregation," collected in a conventicle of very early Georgian design, and unanimously occupied in carrying out the precept of their reverend pastor's text, "Come unto me ... and I will give Rest"—save only those two vigilant old ladies, perhaps pillars of the edifice, and the clerk to whose interest in the sleeping nymph of the next pew I have already alluded—are studies in pure humour.

But to multiply examples of Hogarth's humour would come very near to cataloguing his every work. Let us turn now from that work to the man himself, and study something of those conditions of life of which his genius gives us our most vivid impress.

William Hogarth was born in 1697 or 1698, in London, but of a Westmorland family (Hoggard would seem to have been the earlier spelling), one member of which, the artist's father, after working as a schoolmaster in Westmorland, had settled in London as corrector of the Press.

He must have been a man of some education, since we hear of a Latin-English Dictionary of his composition, though there seems some uncertainty as to whether it ever got beyond the initial stage of MS.; and his son William was early in life bound 'prentice to a silversmith named Gamble, his business being to learn the graving of arms and ciphers upon plate. His marvellous gift for caricature soon showed itself; and a tavern quarrel at Highgate seems to have afforded subject for an early manifestation of his talent in this direction. As the period of his 'prenticeship came to its close he entered an Academy of drawing in St. Martin's Lane, where he may have come under Sir James Thornhill's notice; but seems to have failed to show any exceptional proficiency in his life studies. Form, we have seen already, lay outside—in certain manifestations entirely outside—the peculiar limits of his temperament. Shop-bills and coats-of-arms were probably the mainstay of his livelihood at this period, though plates for books were beginning, little by little, to come in his way; but when in 1730 he clandestinely married the daughter of Sir James Thornhill, the Court painter was so incensed at this mèsalliance that he refused the young couple any acknowledgment. It was at this very time that Hogarth created his first work of individual genius in that superb series of plates to which he gave the name of "The Harlot's Progress"; and it is said that Lady Thornhill designedly placed one of the plates in her husband's way, only to elicit the grudging praise of: "The man who can produce these can also maintain a wife without a portion."

But the ice was broken, and the ensuing thaw led to a complete reconciliation. Sir James Thornhill treated his daughter and son-in-law more generously, and lived with them in future till his death in 1733.

At the same time the Series which had brought about domestic reconciliation, had also brought fame and fortune to the artist. The third scene of the Progress, in which the erring girl is arrested, contained, it would seem, a clever portrait of Sir James Gonson, a magistrate whose energies were famous in this direction. The print is passed around at a meeting of the Board of Treasury, at which Sir James is present; every Lord must repair to the print-shop, to obtain for himself a copy; the vogue was started, and twelve hundred subscribers entered their names for the Series, the price of each set being one guinea.

William Hogarth was now well started in his career of fame; and deservedly so, for in some respects "The Harlot's Progress" is one of the most characteristic and the most brilliant of his creations. Its popularity was immense and instantaneous; it was played in pantomime, and reproduced on ladies' fans. But if he did not surpass the genius of his first invention he certainly came very close to it, both in the "Rake's Progress" and in his "Marriage à la Mode."

Each of these Series, as well as that of the "Industrious and Idle 'Prentices" are complete stories, worked out to their dénoûment—tragedies, one might say, written with a burlesque pencil, of eighteenth-century life. And if the note struck seem sometimes too insistent, if the Industrious one be too sleek, too self-complacent, the prodigal too immersed in sensual folly and indulgence; if the blacks seem too black, and the whites too white, and those half-tones which accord the values of life be generally missing; if a more refined age demands a subtler analysis, a more artistic treatment, can we yet deny the truth and necessity of the eternal lesson? Have we yet reached, or shall we ever reach, an age in which ineptitude, insolence, idleness, fail to work out their inevitable resultant? Or is it less true for us than for those earlier ages—the message which the writer of that magnificent thirty-eighth Psalm reiterates, as though he would drive deep into our souls its lasting verity. "Put thou thy trust in the Lord and be doing good; dwell in the land and verily thou shall be fed. Delight thou in the Lord; and he shall give thee thy heart's desire.... Yet a little while and the ungodly shall be clean gone ... the Lord shall laugh him to scorn, for he hath seen that his day is coming."

Just as insistent, just as certain of his concluding verdict as the Psalmist is the eighteenth-century engraver and humorist. Even his own day may already have seen "the ungodly" set high above men in social position, quoted with respect in financial circles, perhaps even a regular attendant at the local conventicle,—"flourishing," in short, to quote that inimitable phrase of the same Psalmist, "like a green bay-tree"; but he, at least will admit no doubt of the ultimate conclusion. "In all his delineation," says Mr. Austin Dobson,[3] with fine insight, "as in that famous design of Prudhon, we see Justice and Vengeance following hard upon the criminal. He knew, no doubt, as well as we, that not seldom (humanly speaking) the innocent are punished and the guilty go at large. What matter! that message should not be preached by him at any rate. So he drew his 'Bogey' bigger ... and drove his graver deeper in the copper."

Yet it is to be noted that from the first his genius is attracted to social satire. The Masquerades and Operas, Burlington Gate, 1724 (which he calls in his own notes The Taste of the Times)—the first plate which he published on his own account,—was popular enough to be freely pirated. "The Wanstead Assembly" brings him close to the later caricaturists; "The Burning of Rumps" shows us a London crowd beside old Temple Bar, with its ghastly trophies of Jacobite relics; and all these lead up to his later success in the two Progresses and the Marriage Series. In 1733 he had settled in his house in Leicester Fields, with its gilt sign of the Golden Head—the sign which he had fashioned and gilded himself, in the similitude of the painter Van Dyck; and here the most of his life was to be spent, varied by visits in later years to the villa which he then acquired at Chiswick. He is now fairly facing his life work, and a brief survey of this is all we can hope to attempt in the limits of this chapter.

I have already mentioned "The Harlot's Progress," and its immediate successor, "The Rake's Progress," the subjects of which speak for themselves. The country maiden's arrival in London, the breakfast scene with her Jewish admirer, and the scene in Bridewell are to be noted among the prints of the first Series; but all are full of character and interest. In "The Rake's Progress" the second plate introduces us to a side of Hogarth's talent which he was to develop later on more fully in his "Marriage à la Mode"—namely, his satire of eighteenth-century life of fashion.

The awkward youth who in the plate before had come into his fortune is now in the full of its enjoyment: become a fine gentleman, he holds his morning levée of those numerous parasites who minister to his vanity or pleasure. The foreign element (which Hogarth in his heart detested) is here to the front in the figure of the French dancing-master, trying a new step, with the fiddle in his hand; behind him the maître d'armes, Dubois, is making a lunge with his epée de combat, while Figg, a noted English prize-fighter, watches his movements with an expression of contempt. Another portrait is Bridgman, a well-known landscape gardener of the time, who is proposing to our young hero some scheme for his estate; while the seated and periwigged figure who runs his fingers over the harpsichord has been suggested as that of the great composer Handel. But when we start forth to knock down the watch, "beat the rounds," intrigue with the fair, and generally keep up the character of a young blood or "macaroni," a little timely assistance is often welcome; and is here proffered (with hope of due remuneration) by the villainous-looking figure on the prodigal's left, whose recommendation is seen in the letter he presents: "The Capt. is a man of honour, his sword may serve you." Meanwhile, a jockey holds before his master the cup he has won; and a tame poet in the corner seems to be invoking the Muses in unmerited praise of the same patron.

In his next plate Hogarth passes to a scene of indescribable orgy; but all this satire on fashionable extravagance, which we have just noted in detail, is still more fully developed in his masterly Series of "Marriage à la Mode." Hogarth's oil paintings of this complete Series are in the London National Gallery, and it is instructive to compare these with the prints, the two first pictures of the Series being especially attractive in treatment. The second of these, representing the morning, when husband and wife awake to ennui from a night of dissipation, is peculiarly happy in spacing and composition, as my illustration may show; while Plate IV. of this Series, showing a reception of the Countess while at her toilet, gives an opening for a clever satire by our artist of the fashionable society of his day, which is as brilliant as any Venetian scene by Longhi, and the ensuing plates point the sequel to a life of folly. Nor has the artist forgotten here to give a side blow to the foreign element—which aroused his hostility, from the French dancing-master or perruquier to the great Italian Masters—Correggio's "Jupiter and Io" finding a place on the walls of her ladyship's bedroom, just as the "Choice of Paris" had been included in the Rake's levée; and we shall note very soon that these allusions were not incidental, but far more probably intended.

For Hogarth had now in these three series attained a reputation which he probably increased by his delightful studies of pure humour, among which "Modern Midnight Conversation," "The Sleeping Congregation," "Strolling Players in a Barn," "The Laughing Audience," "The Enraged Musician," and "The Distressed Poet" are to be especially commended, as well as that fine series of "The Four Times of the Day," in which last "Morning" (of which I am able to give an illustration) is certainly a masterpiece. His estimate of his own powers had increased, and now led him to leave that path in which his genius had already found its intimate expression, and to seek to become that which he was not and never could be—a great imaginative and historical painter. Without ever having really studied the great Masters of the past, without comprehending either their merits or demerits, he declared that it were an easy task for him to surpass even Correggio on his own ground: the result was, if not disaster, at least something very near to it. The "Sigismunda," which he had painted with the above object, was returned on his hands by the purchaser. It hangs now, indeed, in the National Gallery, but I do not imagine many serious critics will prefer it to the marvellous chiaroscuro, the refined ideal beauty of the Master of Parma. Yet that delicious "Shrimp Girl" which hangs near it, painted with almost a Fragonard's gaiety of palette, shows what our artist might have achieved had he gone, like Morland, for his subjects to the common life of his own country. The staircase paintings of St. Bartholomew's Hospital are not likely, I think, to induce us to revise the above opinion; and Sir Joshua's criticism is here so apposite and so just that I need no excuse for quoting it in some detail. "After this admirable artist had spent the greater part of his life in an active, busy, and, we may add, successful attention to the ridicule of life; after he had invented a new species of dramatic painting in which probably he will never be equalled; and had stored his mind with infinite materials to explain and illustrate the domestic and familiar scenes of common life which were generally, and ought to have been always, the subject of his pencil,—he very imprudently, or rather presumptuously, attempted the great historical style, for which his previous habits had by no means prepared him: he was indeed so unacquainted with the principles of this style that he was not even aware that any artificial preparation was necessary. It is to be regretted that any part of the life of such a genius should be fruitlessly employed."

This criticism, which is all the more telling from its reticence, was keenly felt, and probably never forgiven, by our artist; to us it is of value critically as marking the cleavage between himself and the great English school of the eighteenth century, which sought its inspiration otherwise than in his comedy of life. But with a tenacity, with a stubborn faith in his genius which we cannot but admire, he holds firm to his own view of art. That is in the character of the man—sound, honest, sincere even where he is mistaken or narrow—just as we see him in his self-portrait of the London Gallery, with his faithful "Trump" sitting in front, as who should say, "This is my master, Hogarth—and let me just see the dog who will dare bark at him." And so when his critics barked or railed he held but the more stubbornly to his opinion; he rated the more mercilessly those "black masters," whose faults or whose supreme genius it needed a deeper study than he had given them to understand; and when "Sigismunda," that was to rival Allegri, comes back upon his hands he prices it obstinately at £400, even in his will insisting that it should not be sold below that sum.

But now, not content with attempting to eclipse the great Italian masters, not content with quarrelling with the critics, in the same reckless confidence, with the same bull-dog courage and tenacity he will descend from his artistic charger to meet these last upon their own ground, and armed only with those weapons so dear to them, but new to his untried hands—the goose quill and the ink bottle—will tear down the veil that conceals Beauty, and teach them what in future to write, what to select, what to admire!

I am treating in this chapter William Hogarth as a delineator of the comedy of life, not as an art critic, nor as a philosopher; and it is not my painful duty to drag the gentle reader through the verbose Preface to a no less verbose Introduction, to find ourselves at the end of these still in front of the author's main problem of the "Analysis of Beauty." The work probably suffered from the presence of more than one obliging literary—or would-be literary—friend. We hear of a Mr. Ralph, from Chiswick, volunteering his services in this direction, of a Mr. Nichols following him; and of the

Rev. Mr. Townley being much busied on that Preface, wherein Lomazzo rubs shoulders with Michelangelo and Protogenes, and where the modern mortal hears with astonishment of "the sublime part which is a real je ne sçai quoi," and which, "being the most important part to all connoisseurs, I shall call a harmonious propriety, which is a touching or moving unity, or a pathetic agreement, andc."

But it would be unfair to judge the Analysis by this preface, which admittedly befogged even poor Hogarth himself. Suffice to say here that he seeks to divide his elusive element, which might have defied even the dialectic of Socrates, into its "principles of Fullness, Variety, Uniformity, Simplicity, Intricacy, and Quantity; all which co-operate in the production of beauty, mutually correcting, and restraining each other occasionally"; and that the essay, even if entirely inadequate as a philosophical treatment of the subject, contains many useful suggestions and shrewd observations.

It had been enough surely for one short life-time to have been the greatest pictorial humorist of his age, to have tried to climb above Allegri and Titian, and to have traced in thought Beauty's self to her hidden source; but behold our ill-judged artist plunging now, with equal assurance and courage, into that tumultuous sea of English eighteenth-century political strife. The result was this time fatal to his peace, and probably even to his life. John Wilkes was not a very safe man to attack carelessly, nor yet likely to remain quiescent under this treatment; and Hogarth's print of the "Times," published in September of 1762, provoked a very savage rejoinder in No. 17 of the North Briton. Hogarth's reply was a caricature of the popular leader; who then engaged one of his supporters, named Churchill, to retaliate in an angry epistle to the artist. Hogarth again replies with the graver—that terrible weapon in his practised hands—and draws a portrait of "The Bruiser, once the Reverend Churchill," shown in the form of a dancing bear, with club plastered with lies, and a tankard of porter at his side.

"Never," says one of his earlier critics, "did two angry men with their abilities throw mud with less dexterity; but during this period of pictorial and poetic warfare (so virulent and disgraceful to all the parties) Hogarth's health declined visibly." A presentiment of his end seems to have come to him at his own table among his friends, and he said to them: "My next undertaking shall be the 'End of all things.'" The next day his graver was already busy with the strange plate which he called "The Bathos," where Father Time is seen dying, his broken scythe and hour-glass beside him, amid a chaos of ruin all around.

This was actually his last work, for a month later, on the 28th of October, 1764, having returned in weak health from Chiswick to his house in Leicester Fields, he died suddenly of an aneurysm on his chest. His tomb at Chiswick, where his widow came to join him twenty-five years later (in

1789), was adorned in relief with the mask of Comedy, the wreath of laurel, the palette and the book on Beauty; and it was his friend Garrick who is said to have composed those lines of his epitaph, with which we too may take our farewell of the great artist of comedy:

"... Whose pictur'd morals charm the mind,
And through the eye correct the heart.
If genius fire thee, reader, stay;
If nature touch thee, drop a tear;
If neither move thee, turn away,
For Hogarth's honoured dust lies here."

THE COMEDY OF SOCIETY

In the work of Henry William Bunbury we strike an entirely different note to that of the artist we have just studied. The contrast is, in its way, refreshing as well as instructive. Just as Hogarth appears (b. 1698) at almost the first years of the eighteenth century, so Bunbury dates (b. 1750) from exactly its dividing year; therefore he belongs no longer to those days of Swift and Bolingbroke and Walpole, of Jacobite intrigue and Hanoverian power, but to the period of the American war, and those ominous thunderclouds preceding the French Revolution.

Again, just as William Hogarth belongs entirely to the people, and shares profoundly both their best and worst qualities, so the artist we are now considering belongs no less definitely to the aristocratic class—is a member of a Suffolk family which dated its English origin to the Conquest, which had gained its knighthood from Queen Elizabeth, and its baronetcy from the Merry Monarch; and had himself in his younger days made the "grand tour" of France and Italy, and later held a commission in his Majesty's Militia, and the post of equerry to the Duke of York.

"Something of the amateur"—I have written elsewhere[4]—"remains through all the work of Bunbury, who left politics practically out of his field of subjects, and whose social qualities were one of his greatest charms. He married Catherine Horneck, whose sister Mary had been painted—and, it is said, proposed to—by Sir Joshua Reynolds, who had elsewhere painted these two pretty women together; and when he settled in the country with his young wife, his circle of friends came to include Oliver Goldsmith, the actor Garrick, Hoppner, and Sir Joshua—the latter being godfather to his second son, Henry, and painting his eldest as Master Bunbury in 1781—and last, but not least, Dr. Samuel Johnson." The great Doctor had in fact presented to the young couple their family Bible—a fact which is recorded upon the fly-leaf in our artist's own handwriting. Of the two sons that were born to Henry and Catherine Bunbury, their special hopes seem to have centred on the eldest, Charles John, the lovely child for whom Sir Joshua himself had improvised fairy tales to keep him amused while busy on his portrait; but those hopes were not fulfilled, for his manhood did not bear out the promise of his schooldays, and he died comparatively early.

Bunbury's caricatures commence as early as his foreign tour, though some of the best refer to his later military life in England; especially to the time when he was in camp at Coxheath, during the troubled days of the American War. For we have now left far behind the days of Swift and Bolingbroke and Oxford, of Marlborough's battles, and of the great political settlement which marked the Hanoverian succession. Dettingen and Fontenoy are now old soldiers' tales, and the invasion of England by Charles Stuart, the younger Pretender—in which connection we may remember Hogarth's print of the march of the Guards to Finchley—lies equally behind us: we have passed through the long Ministry of Walpole and that of the elder Pitt, we have seen the war with France, and been stirred by Wolfe's victory and heroic death upon the Heights of Abraham. In a word, we have turned the corner with the year of our artist's birth, and are going downwards into the latter half of the eighteenth century.

George III. has now taken his father's place upon the throne of England: the Tories have returned again to be a power in political life as in the days of Bolingbroke, and against the "King's friends," the party subservient to Court influence, there appears in the nation a very strong democratic movement with John Wilkes as its leader and idol. Meanwhile the fatal policy of Grenville had led to the alienation of the great American colonies, and the passing of the Stamp Act in 1765 brought a complete rupture. But this phase of politics enters but little into our present subject. It is of more interest to inquire, apart from this complex turbulent world of home or foreign politics, what were the people themselves in their home life, their outdoor life, their tastes, aspirations, sympathies, social surroundings? I think we shall get an answer to some of these questions—an answer none the less valuable because it comes to us indirectly—from the study of Henry William Bunbury's social caricatures. These appear to commence with (or are in some special cases even earlier than) his Grand Tour. The delightful "Courier François"—published by Bretherton at 134 New Bond St.—belongs surely to this period; and Thomas Wright, in his valuable "History of Caricature,"[5] seems to bear this out when he says of Bunbury that his earlier prints were etched and sold by James Bretherton, who published also the works of James Sayer—an artist whom we shall meet in our next chapter. In this print the "Courier" cracks a long whip as he covers the ground, mounted upon a steed almost as long, as tough and wiry-looking as himself. A short sword is at his side, and he wears enormous jack-boots. In the distance rise peaked mountains, perhaps those of Southern France or Savoy; and the inn to which he seems bound bears the legend, Poste Royale, with the three fleur-de-lys. Our Courier belongs evidently to the ancien règime, and might indeed have stepped—or galloped—to us out of Sterne's "Sentimental Journey." The drawing of these prints is clumsy and coarse in technique, though full of character; and, in fact, Bunbury, who seems to have begun to publish as early as 1771,[6] when he was only twenty-one years of age, had little knowledge or skill in engraving, and seems, after some preliminary efforts which were not very successful, to have entrusted the most of his work to be engraved by other hands. Thus James Bretherton, who was an engraver as well as a publisher, was engaged on Bunbury's prints from 1772 onwards; though later we shall find Rowlandson working as an engraver on Bunbury's humorous sketches, and necessarily, from his strong individuality, imparting to them much of his own character.

The pendant to the print just described is the "Courrier Anglois," and this was in fact both engraved and published by Bretherton in 1774 (it bears the inscription, H. W. Bunbury, delineavit; J. Bretherton, fecit). In fine contrast to the hurry of the lean Frenchman his English counterpart ambles leisurely along, as if time were for him a matter of entire indifference; his horse is loaded with a heavy pack, against which the rider comfortably leans, while he puts a long horn to his lips. He has no sword, or any weapon of defence; but the two grisly figures by the roadside dangling on a gibbet, and his own inimitable expression of contented ease, seem to imply that travelling is secure for him, and Justice prompt and keen-eyed.

To this period of the Grand Tour belong also, in my judgment, the "Tour to Foreign Parts" (drawn by Bunbury, engraved by Bretherton, published in 1799 by J. Harris of Cornhill), the "Cuisine de la Poste," or "The Kitchen of a French Post House" (H. Bunbury, invt., published 1771 by Harris), "The Englishman at Paris," 1767, the earliest in date of these (Mr. Bunbury, del.; Js. Bretherton, fecit, published 1799 by J. Harris), and lastly the "View on the Pont Neuf at Paris" (H. W. Bunbury, invt. The engraver's name, in my example, is cut). These prints are as precious in their detailed evidence of costume and methods of life as they are amusing. They are snapshots caught—not with a camera, but with an eye and pencil which were almost as quick—of the life of that old monarchic France as it was seen by the English traveller, posting along the great high-roads, or taking his walk through the town. Soon, very soon, all that life was to be swept away in the hurricane of political passion, never in any of its quainter features to return; that is why these jottings of our artist are to the student of this period so inestimably precious.

Our travellers, three in number, and evidently portrayed from the life, have just descended ("A Tour in Foreign Parts") from the two-horse chaise, which the postilion is driving into the yard. The smallest of the three Englishmen, with "Chesterfield's Letters" under his arm, approaches the obsequious host of the "Poste Royale" with a conciliatory smile; the while the landlady is engaged in an assault upon her hen-roost, and the servant-girl seems to aim at a similar result with the domestic cats.

And now ("La Cuisine de la Poste") we are introduced to the interior. The pot-au-feu hangs in the great chimney over the blazing logs; the village gossips are there—the postilion in his clumsy jack-boots, the housewife, and the curé with a friend sipping his glass of red wine—and on the walls Louis le bien-aimé, with baton and perruque, is balanced by Sanctus Paulus, with a sword much bigger than himself, or by the "Ordonnances de Monsieur le Duc de Choiseul, Grand Maître des Postes et Relais de France." Or, again, our travellers have arrived at last in the great city ("Englishman at Paris"), and take their walk in the streets of La Ville Lumiére. A fat monk and a thin peasant seem both to regard our tourist with astonishment; a dandy of the period is driving his chariot with a lackey hanging on behind, and the indispensable perruquier is hurrying to an appointment. Or—in its way most curious of all—we see the Pont Neuf of those old days, with the costumes and characters which then thronged its thoroughfare. Huge muffs seem to have been then the fashion, often combined in use with umbrellas, such as we now should call Japanese sunshades; the perruquier here, too, must have his muff, though both hands are filled with the shaving-pot and curling tongs; the trim abbé in his short cassock, even the truculent-looking postilion are all provided. In the corner a poodle is being clipped, just as we may see to-day beside the Seine, and is loudly vociferating his complaints; and, above all, we see the quaint ensign of the trade, which combined the shoeblack's lower art with that of the dog-barber.

Aux Quarante Lions
St. Louis
Décrotte à l'Anglaise
et Tond des Chiens
Proprement
Allons, Messeigneurs, Allons.

We must turn now to our artist's later prints of English eighteenth-century social life, which are as full of humorous observation, even though they have not the special interest of these notes on old France. For, like Collet and Sandby, his predecessors in English caricature, Bunbury gave but little attention to political caricature. Sandby belongs almost (b. 1725) to the later years of Hogarth's ascendency; and, though not a professional caricaturist, being perhaps annoyed at that artist's depreciation of other painters, many of his caricatures are directed against Hogarth himself. But Sandby's best claim to our interest lies outside our present subject; for his landscape work in steel engraving, in aquatint and oil-colour, had led him up to the discovery of the beauty and interest of water-colour painting, in which art he may claim to be a pioneer. He outlived John Collet, who had been born in the same year (1725) as himself, and is said to have been a pupil of Hogarth, though Lambert, a landscape-painter, is mentioned as giving him his first instructions. Certainly there is something which recalls Hogarth in his drawings, which deal, as I have said, with social satire rather than politics. "A Disaster" treats of a lady who has lost both hat and wig together by the same gust of wind; her footman behind has caught one of these in each hand, and the rustics, who have preserved nature's covering, laugh at her plight. Collet's picture of "Father Paul in his Cups, or The Private Devotions of a Convent," was one of a series by our artist intended to illustrate Sheridan's comedy of "The Duenna," produced in 1775. This was close upon the period of Lord Gordon's riots (1780), and the "No Popery" feeling which then prevailed finds illustration in this work of Collet's. Like Sandby, he worked also in water-colour, and two of his sketches in this medium are mentioned by Bryan as in the Victoria and Albert Museum.

We have now returned with Bunbury from his "grand tour" abroad, and have to study him at his best in his sketches of English social life in town and country. He was probably himself a good horseman, and at any rate understood, as thoroughly as even Caran d'Ache himself, the humorous side of the equestrian art. A whole series of his smaller prints deal with the rider and his steed. "How to pass a carriage," "How to lose your way," "How to travel on two legs in a frost," are among the best of these. Another clever print shows the rider of a pulling animal with a mouth of cast-iron just clearing an old woman's barrow; while among the larger prints we have "Richmond Hill," "Hyde Park," "Coxheath Ho," and "Warley Ho," and his inimitable print of a "Riding House," published by Bretherton in 1780.

Bunbury's caricatures of military subjects naturally connect themselves with the period when he was actively connected with the Suffolk County Militia, more especially when, in 1778, he was in camp at Coxheath at the time of the war in America.

"Recruits," of which I give an illustration, may be included among these, as well as the "Militia Meeting" and "The Deserter," while "A Visit to the Camp" and "A Camp Scene" belong to the same class of subject. The characterisation of "Recruits" is excellent, from the smart young officer to the rustic awkwardness of the two recruits, and the more dangerous self-approval of the third; behind we see a chawbacon grinning at the scene, beneath the portentous sign of "The Old Fortune," with its painting of a wooden-legged and armless veteran. "A Visit to the Camp" gives just such a scene—save that the characters are in eighteenth-century costume—as might be witnessed even to-day, when parents, aunts and cousins visit their young hopeful amid the martial surroundings of his volunteer camp; and here, too, may be mentioned a series of single figures in military costume— a "Life-guardsman," "Light Infantryman," "Light-horseman" and a "Foot-soldier." These were all published by Macklin. The foot-soldier's uniform appears in "Recruits"; the handsome uniform of the Light-horseman, with its plumed helmet and high boots, in "A Visit to the Camp," and again in "The Deserter."

While Bunbury was thus occupied with his military career his wife, whom he had left in lodgings in Pall Mall, gave him their second son, to whom Sir Joshua Reynolds stood godfather. Is it too much to suggest that this latter is the artist caricatured in that delightful "Family Piece," of which I also hope to give an illustration; and which may have been suggested to our artist by the scene in his friend Oliver Goldsmith's masterpiece, "The Vicar of Wakefield"?

To the next period of Bunbury's life—when war's alarms were over and the camp at Coxheath broken up—belong many of his best prints of English country life. He was living now in Suffolk, and his print of the "Country Club" is said to have depicted to the life an institution of that nature in quiet old Bury St. Edmunds; while "Conversazione" and the "Sulky Club" display the social efforts of the period, and his famous "Barber's Shop," which Knight engraved in 1783, comes into this part of his career.

To his visits to the West of England and North Wales about this time we owe some charming sketches—the two "Wynnstay Theatre Tickets," for instance, dating from some visit to Sir Watkin Williams Wynn when theatricals were in the air at Wynnstay, and that lovely print of "The Modern Graces," drawn, it is said, from the three beautiful Misses Shakespere during the stay of our artist at Aston; while those two prints of "Peasants from the Vale of Llangollen" hint at some pleasant ramble in the Welsh hills. Bunbury excelled, in fact, in a class of subject which does not strictly fall within our notice, since we are treating him here as a caricaturist, but which must by no means be neglected by those who appreciate his work.

These are what may be characterised as fancy sketches, which are often, in his hand, singularly graceful and charming in treatment and conception. "The Song," "The Dance," and "Morning Employments" may be mentioned especially among these, all these three having been entrusted to the graver of the famous Bartolozzi. Indeed, in writing of Bartolozzi,[7] I found it impossible to leave Bunbury out of my subject, and said of this artist: "He supplied the engraver with some charming drawings, mostly of English girls in simple country dress—such as the 'Sophia and Olivia,' drawn for Goldsmith's 'Vicar of Wakefield,' where one of the girls touches a guitar and the other holds a roll of music; or, again, that very lovely print, a copy of which is in the Victoria and Albert collection, where three young girls dance hand in hand to the strain which a country lad seated near them is piping. 'The Song,'" I added, "a pendant to this, is no less charming."

"Love and Honour" is another of Bartolozzi's prints from Bunbury, representing a Light-Cavalry soldier taking leave of a pretty country girl, and bearing the legend:

"Hark! the drum commands
Honour! I attend thee!
Love, I kiss thy hands!"

"Lucy of Leinster" and "Bothwell's Lament," it may be noted, are by the same engraver. Apart from its own beauty the engraving of "The Dance" is of especial interest, since the three figures dancing are said to be taken from those famous beauties of the time, the Misses Gunning; and in his "Love and Hope," "Love and Jealousy," and a "Tale of Love," which Bartolozzi's pupil, J. K. Sherwin, engraved for him, he follows with success the same class of subject. It is the sentimental charm, which streams from the fair Angelica Kauffman's pencil and kept busy the best engravers of the time, notably Bartolozzi, Ryland, Sherwin, and Tomkins, which here attracts the soldier and caricaturist, who was also the devoted lover and husband; and in these prints, though the initiative and conception is certainly our artist's, it is difficult to know how much we may not owe to the practised hand of such an engraver as Francesco Bartolozzi.

But certainly this side of art was treated by Henry Bunbury freely, and with marked success, and the list would be a long one if we were to attempt to chronicle all. "Edwin and Ethelinda," "Black-eyed Susan," "Auld Robin Gray" (a charming colour-print, also engraved by Bartolozzi), "Adelaide in the Garden" (by the same engraver), the charming "Songstress," "Charlotte and Werther's meeting," "Margaret's Tomb," "The Girl of Snowdon," "The Girl of Modena," "Marianna," "Cicely," and that sweet "Country Maid" engraved by J. R. Smith in 1782, and whose legend tells us:

"No care but Love can discompose her breast,
Love of all cares the sweetest and the best."

His illustrations to Macklin's Shakespeare come nearer to our subject proper, and here we have the whole Falstaff episode very fully and very humourously illustrated; while Launce and his dog, whom he "would have to behave as a dog at all things," may be compared in our artist's treatment of canine life with his "Black George," the Suffolk gamekeeper.

Was it, we may here ask, in returning to the story of our artist's life, that fatal quality, the artistic temperament, or was it his charming social qualities, his frequent visits to great houses and corresponding expenses, which had brought Henry Bunbury at this time into financial difficulties?

His military connection, which had led to his appointment as A.D.C. to the Duke of York, was too important to be neglected even under these conditions.

Hence it is that in 1788 we find the Bunburys settled in London at Whitehall. Our artist was now, from his Court position and his own tastes, thrown into the midst of London social life; and this new life in all its features begins to reproduce itself in his caricatures. "Hyde Park," "The Coffee House Patriots," "The Chop House," "Richmond Hill," "Bethnal Green," and the large print of a "Fête at Carlton House" (at which no doubt he was present in attendance on the Duke), belong to this period of his life.

Bath he no doubt knew well already from his visits to the West of England, where it was at this time the great rendezvous for fashionable society; he must have himself moved in this society, and enjoyed the study of its follies and foibles, its airs and graces, which the dramatists of the time love to reproduce. For here certainly it was that he gained his inspiration for the "Long Minuet," as danced at Bath, with its line of stately dancers and its classical inscription—

"Longa Tysonum minuit
Quid velit et possit rerum concordia discors."

This is one of Bunbury's most famous prints; and justly so, for nothing could be truer to life, especially to eighteenth-century life, and probably to Bath of the period, than these bowing and pirouetting figures.

In his "Lumps of Pudding" we have the same theme, but treated with a coarser note; and yet some of the figures are excellent—notably the stout gentleman in the corner, who has removed his wig to mop his heated brow—the enthusiast near him who is "setting" before a dame with a three-decker and its anchor in her hair, and the group of four who are next the lady dancing with her pet dog. The "Long Minuet" and this last belong to that class of caricatures in which the figures form a continued story—a line of humour which the Germans have developed in Fliegende Blätter, which Caran d'Ache has used with success in France, and which Pick-Me-Up, when it was under the able direction of Mr. Leslie Willson, scored many a good point with.

Lord Derby

LORD DERBYTo this class, too, belongs Bunbury's famous "Propagation of a Lie," published in 1787. Male figures only appear in this wonderful series; though (alas!) many of us have learnt from experience that the fair sex, with all its charm, is not always averse to "broder" the simple truth, especially when a prospect of scandal is concerned. Bath, we may feel sure, would have offered in those days every facility of this nature, if required; and it may be fairly assumed that the mise-en-scène for this print was the same as that of the "Long Minuet." From "Dear me! You don't say so!" we proceed through the stages of "Heigh ho!" "O fye!" "Indeed!" "There now!" to that lively dandy who exclaims "Ha! Ha!" and that irascible old gentleman who is shaking his fist at him with the reply, "God's zounds! hold your tongue!" To the same line of social satire belong the "Front, side, and back view of a modern Gentleman," "Sunday Evening," "Morning, or the Man of Taste," and "Evening, or the Man of Feeling" (engraved by J. R. Smith in 1781), and a "Fashionable Salute," called "Salutation Tavern," of which I give a plate from the print in my own collection. The same engraver, J. R. Smith, produced Bunbury's sketch of "Lord Derby on Horseback," following the coach of the lovely Miss Farren,[8] which has the motto:

"When I followed a lass that was froward and shy."

But the "lass" in question became less shy later, and complied to his request to become Countess of Derby.

"Patience in a Punt," one of our artist's best-known prints, was engraved by Rowlandson, and has acquired a good deal of his characteristic drawing in the process; and I may mention briefly here some prints dealing with Cambridge life—"The Hope of the Family," "Admission at the University," and "Pot Fair, Cambridge" (dated 1777), as well as a series of very interesting original etchings by our artist in the British Museum collection. Professor Colvin tells me that a recently acquired collection there of Italian prints included several by Bunbury; and among these may have been "John Jehu—L'Inghilterra," 1772, and "The Dog-Barber—La Francia," 1772 (a theme which we have noted in his print of the "Pont Neuf"), as they by their titles seem to be evidently intended for the Italian market. By far the most interesting, in one way, of these etchings by our artist—which date from the beginning of his career and are often very weak in drawing—is one which shows two boys, or men, one of whom is riding a pig; and which belongs to the time when Bunbury was a boy at Westminster School, being thus, as I believe, his earliest existing caricature. The British Museum is, in fact, very rich in Bunbury's prints; and his series there of the "Arabian Nights" (in colour, engraved by Ryder) may be noted here (the print of "Morgiana's Dance" being especially charming), ere we turn back to our artist's life story. In 1797 the Bunburys had taken a small house at Oatlands, near Weybridge, to be near the Duke and Duchess of York, who were then residing at Oatlands Park; and it was here that in 1798 Henry Bunbury had a terrible blow, in the loss of his wife at the early age of forty-five years. The beautiful face and figure of Catherine Horneck had often appeared in our artist's fancy subjects; their life together seems to have been a very happy one, and we may believe that he never entirely recovered from this loss, for the next thirteen years of his life after her decease were spent by him in comparative retirement. He left Oatlands, and probably also, then or later, his official post at Court, and came to live in the Lake Country, where he had Robert Southey as his friend; it was at Keswick that he died, in 1811, and lies buried there far away from the grave of his wife in Weybridge Church.

His prints form a link in our knowledge of eighteenth-century social life in

England which we could ill afford to lose. Not always very strong in drawing, his humour is genuine, wholesome, spontaneous; his sense of beauty, in subjects outside of pure caricature, often very fascinating and refined; while in both classes of subject he remains happily free from that coarseness which disfigures to some extent the great caricaturists whom I shall treat of in my next two chapters. A charming personality—all his work seems to tell us—and a lovable man; English to the core, in the best sense, fond of his home, fond of outdoor life, fond of his joke, but a joke whose laughter has no bitterness or malice, and leaves no bad taste behind.

THE COMEDY OF POLITICS

In treating here of English eighteenth-century caricature, I find that the conditions of space at my command in this work compel me, in order to do my subject any justice at all, to focus my reader's interest on certain central figures, who typify, each in themselves, one side or other of their art; and to pass by more slightly some of the lesser men, whose interest is either divided or secondary.

Such a towering personality in caricature as James Gillray comes necessarily into the first of these categories; such draughtsmen as Woodward or Sayer into the second.

Woodward comes near to Bunbury in style and subject, and like him seems to have preferred social satire, though occasionally—as in his "General Complaint," of 1796—he touches political topics of the time. Sayer, belonging to the period of Gillray, is, like him, essentially a political caricaturist. James Sayer was the son of a merchant captain, and had been put to the profession of attorney: but caricature attracted him more than law, and, having gained the notice and interest of the younger Pitt, he attached himself to his service with such industry and success that Charles James Fox is said to have remarked that Sayers' caricatures had cost him more votes than all the speeches in the House of Commons.

In fact, just as certain modern English politicians,—Lord Palmerston in earlier days, and, in later, Mr. Gladstone and Mr. Joseph Chamberlain—seem to have been singled out (a compliment this to the public interest in their personality) as especial targets for the caricaturist's shaft, so Fox was throughout the object of Sayer's constant devotion. His first effort was directed against the Rockingham Ministry of 1782; but far happier was his "Paradise Lost," published on the fall of that Administration, which shows the once happy pair, Fox and Burke, turned away from their previous

Paradise, the Treasury, over whose gate appears the menacing head of Lord Shelburne—who succeeded them at the head of the Cabinet, Pitt being Chancellor of the Exchequer—with others of his Ministerial colleagues above ...
... "the gate
With dreadful faces thronged and fiery arms.
Some natural tears they dropt, but wiped them soon;
The world was all before them, where to choose
Their place of rest, and Providence their guide."
James Gillray made his entry into English political caricature almost at the same date as Sayer—namely in 1782—with his caricatures on the subject of Rodney's naval victory. His father was of Scotch descent, and having been wounded as a soldier at the battle of Fontenoy—where he lost his arm—he became in later life an out-pensioner of Chelsea Hospital; so that it was in Chelsea that James, his son, was born. Like William Hogarth he too was put in his early years to letter engraving; but, becoming tired of this rather dull employment, he ran away and joined a company of strolling players, sharing in the hardships and adventures of their roving life, perhaps taking part in such scenes as Hogarth had depicted in his famous print, where the company have successfully "stormed" their barn and are getting ready— dressing-rooms being at a discount—for the next performance.
But Gillray's bent towards the plastic arts must have been too strong to let him remain long in the theatre: when he returned to London he became a student of the Royal Academy, and seems to have worked hard at improving his drawing. He also studied under the engraver Bartolozzi; and the result of his training begins to show itself in his engravings of "The Deserted Village" and "The Village Train," published in 1784 to illustrate Goldsmith's poem, and in his imitations of drawings by Lavinia, Countess Spencer. But, though successful as an engraver, and even as a painter, it was as a caricaturist that he was destined to win his lasting fame. Here his individuality came at once to the front; though even when a professional caricaturist he continued the practice of engraving and painting, as his portraits of William Pitt and numerous engravings bear witness.
The political history of England was then approaching a most dramatic epoch, and this—even apart from Gillray's marvellous natural aptitude in this direction—might well have tempted him to choose politics as his special subject. The French and American wars had scarcely yet left men's memories; a King was on the throne who had joined to no great political sagacity or insight a stubborn determination to govern; and the clash of political issues, the struggle of the two great traditional English parties, was intensified and rendered more brilliant by the figures of famous statesmen or orators—such as Pitt, Fox, Burke, and Sheridan, and, but in a lesser degree, Thurlow and Shelburne.

But yet further, before this very generation the tremendous and (as we shall see it to have been) world-absorbing spectacle of the French Revolution was to unrol itself, touching every individual in his most intimate interests and convictions, awaking everywhere feelings of passionate enthusiasm, or of corresponding hatred; and then, gradually, out of that sea of blood which we know in history as the Terror, the sinister form of Buonaparte, General, Consul, Dictator, Emperor, came to detach itself, to blot out all lesser figures, to become a menace to the world. All this had passed before the eyes of Gillray and his fellow-countrymen. He saw the thundercloud arise that was to darken the horizon. He saw the energy and genius of Pitt create one Coalition after another, only to find them melt away before the victorious armies of France. He saw at length—and his trumpet-call at that crisis gave no uncertain sound—England stand alone, and find in herself the forces that were to bring her safely through the storm.

We have noted already Sayers' caricature of the triumph of the Shelburne Ministry in 1782; a print which had been followed by his still more clever satire—called "Carlo Khan's Triumphant Entry into Leadenhall Street"— on Fox's India Bill of 1783. In that same year Shelburne's Ministry had been overthrown, and Fox and Burke came back into office with Lord North. Against these statesmen, whether in or out of office, Gillray's pencil became largely employed, though he was never a hired caricaturist or kept in fee like Sayer, and all sides of politics (including the Court and even the King himself) felt the edge of his satire; while Lord Thurlow, the great Lord Chancellor, was in no way neglected. Thus we find a "New Way to pay the National Debt" (1786), "Ancient Music" (1787), "Monstrous Craws" (1787), "Frying Sprats" (1791) and "Anti-Saccharites, or John Bull and his Family leaving off the use of Sugar" (1792), are all directed against the reigning House, and allude frequently to the parsimonious habits of George III. and his Queen. The story goes that this monarch, having remarked of Gillray's drawings, "I don't understand these caricatures," the artist drew him ("A Connoisseur Examining a Cooper," 1792) studying minutely with a glass the miniature of Oliver Cromwell, remarking at the time: "I wonder if the Royal Connoisseur will understand this?"

But if the economy of the King was a subject for his satire, the opposite qualities in the Prince of Wales met with as little mercy. "The Voluptuary under the Horrors of Digestion" (1792) gives a very clever treatment of this latter theme; and in a "Morning after Marriage, or a Scene upon the Continent," we seem to find the same distinguished person, with a lady who may be the charming Mrs. Fitzherbert.

About this period, too, Lord Thurlow, in a "Westminster Hunt" (1788) and "Market Day" (also 1788, where the motto, "Every man his price," seems aimed at the fat kine of the House of Commons), is not forgotten; while in "Dido Forsaken," where the Queen of France stands deserted and desperate on her own shores, and Fox and his friends in a row-boat are steering for Dover Castle with the remark, "I never saw her in my life!" ("No! never in his life, damme!" adds Fox at the rudder), we seem to be already getting drawn into the mäelstrom of the French Revolution. Perhaps to the average student the period of Gillray's work which we are here approaching will be of most interest, because a fairly exact knowledge of English party politics is necessary to follow with enjoyment his earlier prints on home affairs. Gillray had treated a French subject with success in his amusing "Landing of Sir John Bull and his Family at Boulogne-sur-Mer," which recalls Bunbury to our thought both in its humour and treatment. This latter artist had thoroughly appreciated James Gillray's genius, and said of his great contemporary that "he was a living folio, every page of which abounded with wit."

Following the order of time, which is perhaps our safest guide, "The Bengal Levée" is a large print, full of clever portraits, "made on the spot by an Amateur"; and "The Dagger Scene, or the Plot discovered," is a political print which must not be omitted. But now we find ourselves suddenly launched into the midst of the French Revolution in "French Liberty and British Slavery" (showing a starving Jacobin praising his own Government, and a fat John Bull at dinner abusing his); and "Sansculottes feeding Europe with the Bread of Liberty," this latter a most inimitably clever print, whose centre is formed by John Bull, with Fox and a sympathiser administering the Bread of Liberty on the dagger's point, while Germany, Holland, and Italy are at the corners.[9] Gillray had already, as we see here, taken a strongly anti-French attitude, which he never altered, and which, no doubt, faithfully reflected the mass of English public opinion, horrified at the excesses with which Paris had in those days sullied the pure name of Liberty. I say advisedly the mass, for Charles James Fox next appears in "Dumourier dining in State at St. James's" (1793), serving up to the French General the head of Pitt upon a dish, with the British crown thrown in as an entremet. A very striking print of the same year shows the heroic "Charlotte Corday upon her Trial" (July 17, 1793), and a figure very like Gillray's usual rendering of Talleyrand, with two other judges, upon the bench beneath the cap of Liberty. "The Blessings of Peace and the Curses of War," with its inscription—"Such Britain was, such Flanders, Spain and Holland now is (sic); from such a sad reverse, O Gracious God, preserve our country!"—is an eloquent, if slightly ungrammatical, appeal (Jan. 17, 1795) to his fellow-countrymen, an appeal to which our artist must have been stirred by the horrible carnage and misery which the French armies were then inflicting upon the continent of Europe; while "John Bull ground down" (June 1, 1795) shows the guineas being extracted from that long-suffering person, despite his cries of "Murder"; and in "Blind-man's Buff, or Too Many for John Bull" (June 12, 1795) he is being handed over, with

Pitt's assistance, to the kicks and plunder of the Powers of Europe.

The Jacobin Drummer

THE JACOBIN DRUMMERWe reach the full horrors of the Terror in Paris, and trace its effect on outside opinion, in a very clever print in my own possession entitled "Promised Horrors of the French Invasion, or Forcible Reasons for Neglecting a Regicide Peace." The print is so full of masterly detail that it almost defies description. In the centre a figure (? that of Pitt) is being flogged by Fox beneath the Tree of Liberty, planted at the Piccadilly end of St. James's Street, with three human thigh-bones at its base; beside it the French troops march up St. James's Street, leaving the Palace in smoke and flames, and invade White's Club on their right, pitching its ill-fated members on to the bayonets in the street, but are received by the members of Brookes's Club on their left with cries of welcome, and a set of heads neatly arranged upon a plate, with the motto, "Killed for the Public Good!" October 20, 1796, is the date of this magnificent cartoon of our artist, which must have found an echo in public opinion: but ships, troops, and subsidies mean taxation, and Pitt's continued demands on the Treasury are satirised in "The Nuptial Bower" (February 15, 1797) and "Political Ravishment, or The Old Lady of Threadneedle Street in Danger" (May 22, 1797).

In the year following (1798) the form of Nelson makes its appearance in the print of "The British Hero cleansing ye Mouth of ye Nile," and in "John Bull Taking a Luncheon"—off a captured French three-decker.

For now, too (November 21, 1799), the figure of Buonaparte, which was to occupy so fully Gillray's pencil, makes his entry into these caricatures in the cartoon of "Exit Liberté, a la Francois (sic) or, Buonaparte closing the Farce of Egalité at S. Cloud, near Paris, November 16, 1799."

Another print, however, touching the Directorate period is too important to be entirely omitted from our list. It is called "Ci-devant Occupations, or Madame Tallien and the Empress Josephine dancing naked before Barras in the Winter or 1797—a Fact." The dancers can be traced behind a veil of gauze, while Barras sits at table, very drunk, beneath an infant Bacchus wearing the Cap of Liberty, and Buonaparte watches the scene from the side in front of a pile of skulls. "Madame Tallien," we are here informed, "is a beautiful woman, tall and elegant: Josephine is smaller and thin, with bad teeth"; in which case she must be the figure nearest Buonaparte, and must have gone up in weight—in Gillray's view—before she appears in his "Handwriting on the Wall."

It would be impossible within the limits of this series to give a detailed list of all the superb series of Gillray's satires on the Napoleonic struggle. I have been fortunate enough to obtain for this work reproductions of three among the best ones; but my account may do well to commence with that delightful print (another hit at Charles James Fox) of the "Introduction of

Citizen Volpone and his Suite at Paris"; might note further "The Vexation of Little Boney"; and strike a higher note in "The Handwriting upon the Wall," where, in the hour of his triumph, Buonaparte, seated at table beside an enormously stout Josephine, with gigantic and savage-looking Guards and very décolletées and ringleted maids-of-honour waiting in service on them, sees with dilated eyes on the wall the warning of his doom.

Of course the threatened invasion of England finds its echo in Gillray's prints. "French Invasion, or Buonaparte Landing," "Armed Heroes" (of which I give here a reproduction), and the "King of Brobindnag and Gulliver" all belong to this theme of the nation's peril; as does that interesting print, which I also reproduce, of "Britannia between Death and the Doctor," where the sick lady is threatened on the one side by Buonaparte as Death, the while Pitt, as chief physician, executes a war dance at the expense of his professional rivals, planting his heel very neatly in the mouth of the prostrate Charles James Fox. Napoleon's European victories find comment in the "Surrender of Ulm," and in another of my plates, "Tiddy Doll, the Great French Gingerbread Maker, drawing out a New Batch of Kings," where Talleyrand seems, very appropriately, to be the figure in the background kneading the dough (note, too, the rubbish heap). But the worst danger was past already at the time (as we know now) of that fine plate that commemorates the "Death of Admiral Lord Nelson in the Moment of Victory," published by Humphrey of St. James Street, on December 23, 1805.

Gillray, after trying various publishers—Kent, Brown, Holland of Oxford Street, Fores of Piccadilly—seems to have settled down with Humphrey, first in the Strand, then in Bond Street, and later St. James Street, whose shop-windows became famed for his prints. Joseph Grego, a known authority on our artist, relates that Fox and Burke once walked into the shop together, alarming the worthy proprietress by this sudden invasion of Gillray's favourite subjects. But Burke reassured her with a smile: "Were I to prosecute you it would be the making of your fortune; and that favour, excuse me, Mrs. Humphrey, you do not entirely merit at my hands."

We may terminate our study or Gillray's Napoleonic caricatures very appropriately with the "Spanish Bullfight," in which Buonaparte is tossed by the Spanish bull (Peninsular War of 1808) before the assembled Powers of Europe (dated July 11, 1808); and the fine print of the "Valley of the Shadow of Death" (September 24, 1808), in which the prediction of an earlier print ("The Handwriting on the Wall") seems near its fulfilment, and the Powers of Europe in grim demonic shapes surround the terrified ruler, the British lion charging him full in front, while the Russian bear takes an ugly snatch from behind at his legs.

James Gillray's political caricatures are so interesting and so important, they form such a priceless commentary on the history of the time, that I have given them the priority of space over his amusing social satires, which scourge without mercy the follies of dress and fashion. "A Lady putting on her Cap" (1795), "Lady Godiva's Rout" (1796), "High Change in Bond Street" (1796), "A Modern Belle at Bath" (1796), and "A Fashionable Mamma" come into this class, as well as "Following the Fashion," "Characters in High Life," and many others. It was the epoch when English ladies' waists seem to have risen nearly to their arm-pits, and when their hair towered up correspondingly into a forest of feathers; and all the above prints—as well as the series of "Faro's Daughters," directed at the gambling craze, "The Graces in a High Wind (as seen from Nature in Kensington Gardens)," and the still more risky series of "Three Stages of a Lady's Toilet,"—depict these extreme fashions.

"Tales of Wonder," "Advantages of Wearing Muslin Dresses, dedicated to the Fashionable Ladies of Great Britain," "A Broad Hint of not Meaning to Dance," "A Company shocked at a Lady getting up to Ring the Bell," belong to a slightly later period of costume, say 1802-04.

"Dido in Despair" is evidently a satire on the beautiful Lady Hamilton, who is however represented in this print as enormously fat.[10] Gillray has evidently no sympathy or mercy for the frail and famous beauty; for here she is tumbling out of bed in nightcap and nightdress, from which a huge foot protrudes, while she waves her fat arms in despair. A flask of Maraschino is on the dressing-table near the rouge pot; on the floor lie broken antiques; and a work on Studies of Academic Attitudes, with scarcely academic illustrations, lies near the window, through which is seen a line of British battleships standing out to sea.

"Ah where and oh where is my gallant sailor gone?

He's gone to fight the Frenchmen for George upon the throne,"—

is the motto of this print, which was published by Humphrey on February 6 of 1801. "The Bulstrode Siren" (Mrs. Billington), where she is seen warbling to the Duke of Portland, fares little better than Emma herself; and Sir William Hamilton appears, in another of Gillray's satires, as "A Conoscenti contemplating ye beauties of ye Antique." Among these last objets d'art a battered "Lais" and a "Bacchante" who has lost her head seem as full of cryptic allusion as the dancing figures on a Greek vase and the Cupid with a bent arrow; while quite in Hogarth's best vein is the "Mark Antony" framed upon the wall, in a cocked hat and admiral's uniform, the "Cleopatra" with a gin bottle, and a view of Vesuvius in full eruption.

Sheridan is a frequent figure in Gillray's political caricatures; but perhaps he was never more happily treated than when he enters as Harlequin, armed with a goose quill, and assisted by John Kemble and the famous Mrs. Siddons, in "Blowing up the Pic Nics." To the same class and subject of satire belongs the "Pic Nic Orchestra" and "Dilettante Theatre"—this last a Green-room scene which seems reminiscent of Hogarth's print of a similar subject. "Two-penny Whist" and "Push-pin" are filled with contemporary portraits;[11] and the two series of "Cockney Sportsmen" (4 plates, 1800) and "Elements of Skating" (4 plates, 1805) must not be overlooked any more than such weirdly hideous creations as "Comfort to the Corns," as "Begone dull Care, I prithee," and "The Gout."

Interesting, however, though much of Gillray's social satire certainly is, it scarcely reaches the same level as his political work. He was a magnificent engraver, and was able in his best time to build up his cartoon with the smallest possible scaffolding, a few lines pencilled upon a card being enough to enable him to commence at once upon the copper; while the freedom and facility of his design is witnessed amply by all his prints— those prints which we have now studied in some measure together, though anything in the nature of a comprehensive catalogue is denied me by the space at my command. His influence, too, upon Isaac Cruikshank is to be marked, as a link in the evolution of English caricature.

In his later years James Gillray resided almost entirely with his kindly publisher, Mrs. Humphrey, of whom, as I have noted, he has left a whimsical portrait, with her faithful maid "giggling Betty," in his print of "Two-penny Whist." Mrs. Humphrey appreciated her client's genius, and at one time their mutual understanding got so far on the road to matrimony that they had already reached the door of the church (their parish church of S. James, Piccadilly) when this eccentric bridegroom remarked, "This is a foolish affair, Mrs. Humphrey. We live very comfortably together—better let well alone!"—and walked home to work on his copper plate. But even if this legend of blighted hopes be correct, the good spinster in any case devoted herself no less to the artist's comfort and welfare; and the tragedy of his later years was due to himself alone. Intemperance weakened his powers; and in the last years of his life he lapsed, from this cause probably, into a condition of mental imbecility, which contrasts sadly with those busy and successful years of his life, from 1777 to close on 1810.

He died upon the 1st of June, 1815, and was buried near the rectory of S. James, Piccadilly; within reach of the busy roar of that London whose complex multitudinous life he had lived amongst and loved and studied, and which still surges around his last resting-place in changed and ever-changing forms.

THE COMEDY OF LIFE

Thomas Rowlandson, the last and in some ways the greatest of the caricaturists whose work illustrates the eighteenth century, was born in London in 1756, being thus just six years younger than Bunbury, and one year older than Gillray; so that all these artists cover very much the same period, although their work has elements of the greatest diversity.

In Bunbury we have seen the really gifted amateur, who entrusted his clever sketches to other hands to be engraved, who kept in touch with social life in London and county society, and pursued his career in the army and at Court, while throughout devoting himself to art as his greatest hobby. Again, later, we have traced briefly Gillray's supreme talent, both as engraver and draughtsman, more especially in his magnificent series of contemporary political cartoons. But in Rowlandson we touch a genius as fertile, but of a different order, and, I incline to think, of a considerably wider grasp; and if I call this chapter, which I am devoting especially to his work, the "Comedy of Life"—in contrast to pictorial morals, to society or politics—it is because life in all its exuberance, all its variety and fertility, seems to stream on us from the gifted artist's pencil.

But Life contains—thanks be—not only coarse, distorted types of humanity, exaggerations of foolish fashion, and political antagonisms, but grace and beauty, even with the changing form of the time-spirit; and it is just here that Rowlandson infinitely surpasses those contemporaries whom we studied in our last chapter. His female figures have often that rich English beauty which we find in Reynolds, Hoppner, or sometimes in Morland; and his landscape has qualities of very exceptional merit. He might, we are frequently tempted to think, have been a painter worthy to take a front rank even in that magnificent English eighteenth-century school, which included Reynolds, Gainsborough, Romney, Hoppner, among its glories; but as we come to study his life we shall find in the insouciance of his character, in the very facility of his genius, the causes which made him—not, indeed, entirely to our loss—only the greatest caricaturist of his time.

As a boy already, at Dr. Barrow's academy in Soho, he had attracted notice by his humorous sketches of his fellow pupils; and in his sixteenth year he went to Paris at the invitation of his aunt, a Mlle. Chatelier, with the object of pursuing art study in that city. He had already been admitted as a student in the Royal Academy; and his life studies in Paris are said to have possessed great merit. Paris itself at this time (about 1772-4), with Louis XV. still on the throne, must have been very fascinating to the young English lad, living with a relative who treated him with affection and generosity, in the first consciousness too of his genius, in the midst of a most brilliant capital, and with every prospect of fortune waiting for him. These years left, without doubt, an indelible impression on his mind. Mr. Grego, an authority on this artist as well as Gillray, expresses this[12] very happily when he says: "It was the more romantic Paris of Sterne that Rowlandson first viewed, and he seems to have recognised and noted down the characteristics of the same typical personages described by 'Yorick'; their two satirical points of view were identical. It was indeed the ideal artistic centre: Fragonard, Lavrience, Eisen, St. Aubin, and the school of followers of Boucher and Lancret—elegant triflers in their way, but unequalled for dash and brilliancy—were the leading spirits as Rowlandson imbibed his first inspiration from these attractive fonts. His two years' residence in the midst of these appetising surroundings must have been the happiest of Rowlandson's career; the seeds sown amid these gayer scenes blossomed forth in later years, and influenced the artist in gradually devoting his gifts from the dull routine of portrait-painting to the indulgence of his fruitful imagination."

Whether indeed all the influence which the critic here mentions was entirely for good, is, I think myself, open to question. It is quite possible that our artist acquired at this time the taste for gambling which led him to the brink of ruin more than once in later life; and I have suggested already that had he kept to painting he might have achieved in that medium a fame far above even that which he now possesses. For on his return to London he resumed his studies at the Royal Academy Schools, and in 1775 exhibited at the Academy "Samson visited by Delilah," which he followed up by the portraits on which he was busy now in Wardour Street from 1778 to 1781. His work must have shown considerable power to be hung beside the canvases of Reynolds, Romney, and Hoppner; but at the later date of 1784 his exhibited drawings—"Vauxhall Gardens," "The Serpentine," and "An Italian Family"—show already a tendency to the lighter side of art, and between the above date and 1787 the direction of his art has changed in favour of caricature.

His imagination was as fertile as his pencil was facile. The market was easy—Fores (for whom Gillray also worked), Ackermann,[13] and others offering a ready sale for his satires; and, since we are treating of him here as a caricaturist, it is at this point that we must take his work in detail. The purely humorous prints commence as early as 1781 ("The Village Doctor," published in June of that year by Humphrey), and are followed up (November 27, same year and publisher) by "Charity Covereth a Multitude of Sins," and that unpleasing subject (published by Fores, 1783) of "The Amputation"; but it is in his political cartoons of 1784—such as "Britannia roused, or the Coalition Monster destroyed"—that we begin to recognise the distinctive touch of Thomas Rowlandson. This vigorous print shows a half-draped female figure catching Charles James Fox by the ankle and Lord North by the throat; in this print he takes the same political attitude as his contemporary Gillray, whom he resembles, though far less virulently, in his anti-French prints, while he shows less marked hostility to the reigning house.

The famous Westminster election of the same year (1784) brought Rowlandson still further into political satire, in which Charles James Fox and the beautiful Georgina, Duchess of Devonshire, are leading figures. In "The Devonshire, or the most approved manner of securing votes," the lovely duchess is bestowing a warm embrace on a voter, in the shape of a fat butcher, while another lady, perhaps the Duchess of Gordon, looks on approvingly with the words "Huzza! Fox for ever!" In the "Lords of the Bedchamber," Georgina, seated in her boudoir beneath Reynolds' portrait of her duke, is entertaining to tea two privileged visitors, Fox and his leading supporter, Sam House—"brave, bald-headed Sam" as he was then called. The enthusiastic support which her Grace gave to Fox's candidature gave an opening which was used—often too freely—by the caricaturists. In "Wit's last stake, or the Cobbler's vote," she is seated upon Fox's knee, the while a cobbler puts a stitch into her shoe, so that she may have the excuse of pouring a handful of guineas into his wife's hand. In another print she appears neglecting the infant heir of the Cavendishes for a fox, dressed up in baby clothes; and upon Fox's triumphant return is made by the artist to carry him pick-a-back, and to stop at Mungo's Hotel for a drop of gin.

It is but fair to our Caricaturist to say that the fair Pittite champion, Lady Buckingham, is treated no less mercilessly; and that, even while he was aiming the most outrageous shafts of ridicule and innuendo at the Duchess, his pencil did justice to her extraordinary beauty and charm, both in the prints above mentioned, and in a "Procession to the Hustings after a successful Canvass," in which she leads the way in a big picture hat, and carrying a perfectly indescribable ensign with "The Man of the People" as its legend. Finally, "The Westminster Mendicant" and the "Westminster

Deserter drummed out" complete this really brilliant series of election caricatures, of which I have only detailed the most interesting. In the last-named print it is "brave baldheaded" Sam House who beats the drum, while on his left is the triumphant candidate, Charles James Fox, who addresses the crowd with the time-hallowed words, "Friends and fellow citizens, I cannot find words to express my feelings, etc.," and on his right the defeated Sir Cecil Wray; while behind are the Irish chairmen who had fought (in every sense of the word) so lustily for Fox, and a procession of London maidservants, armed with mops and brooms.

In my account of this series of prints (which all fall within the dates of April and May of 1784) I shall note briefly one remaining print, "For the Benefit of the Champion," in which Fox and Lord North, in female attire, and the Duchess in her large picture hat, but décollettée, and with bare arms, are busy singing a dirge on the defeated opponent. Georgina, a figure of delicious sprightliness and beauty, points to the tombstone marked "Here lies poor Cecil Ray," while the spectacled profile of Burke peeps into the door. And here I may remark again how astonishingly to my own experience a study of these prints makes history real, vivid, and living. These dry bones of bygone politics become clothed with flesh; and names which we had studied with colder interest become friends, and almost intimates. Ere we leave the theme of politics, it may be noted that in the great French War Rowlandson does not come behind Gillray in his patriotic enthusiasm. A whole series of prints, from July to September 1808, was directed against Napoleon; while Nelson appears in a print of which, by the kindness of its possessor, Mr. Newman, a great collector of Nelson relics, I am able to give a plate—"Admiral Nelson recruiting with his brave tars after the glorious Battle of the Nile" (published by Ackermann, October 20, 1798); and both contemporary figures are alluded to in "Napoleon Buonaparte in a Fever on Receiving the Astounding Gazette of Nelson's Victory over the Combined Fleets" (Ackermann, November 13, 1805).

But it is time for us to betake ourselves to Rowlandson's social caricatures, which after all represent the best of his life work; and I am tempted to quote—in seeking illustration of that wonderful sense of life which seems to stream upon us from his pencil—some words of my own in an earlier work, in which I had occasion to treat of this artist. "These creatures of his scenes of comedy—drawn boldly in outline with the reed pen dipped in Indian ink and vermillion, with the shadows then washed in, and the whole slightly tinted in colour—seem full-blooded, vigorous, overflowing with animal life and energy. His women above all are delicious. Rather voluptuous, perhaps, and full in form, but yet indescribably charming in their mob caps, or those big 'picture' hats that George Morland loved, in the tight sleeves and high-waisted gowns falling in long folds about their limbs—their eyes sparkling with roguery, and their whole being breathing the charm of sex."[14]

We may commence our study of his social satires here, in following to some extent the sequence of time, with "A Sketch from Nature"—published by J. R. Smith in January of 1784, and engraved by him in stipple with great beauty and finish. The subject here recalls a very similar scene in Hogarth's "Rake's Progress," for here, as there, a merry company of both sexes is engaged in riotous revel; and the wine and punch flowing freely has got into the heads, and found expression in the behaviour, of the nymphs and their attendant swains. "Money-lenders," "Councillor and Client," and "Bookseller and Author" (all 1784) are excellent character-studies of male figures: the eighteenth century evidently needed the presence of Sir Walter Besant, for the bookseller is fat, prosperous, and overbearing, the author terribly thin, poorly dressed, and looking overworked. In "The Golden Apple or the Modern Paris" (1785) the fair Georgina again appears before us with her rival beauties, the Duchesses of Rutland and Gordon:

"Here Juno Devon, all sublime,
Minerva Gordon's wit and eyes,
Sweet Rutland, Venus in her prime."

The three ladies appear before the Prince of Wales, afterwards George the Fourth—the "Modern Paris" who has the difficult task of awarding the apple. The Prince re-appears in Rowlandson's famous print of "Vauxhall Gardens" (published by J. R. Smith in 1785) with a star upon his breast, where he is paying much attention to Mrs. Robinson—the lovely "Perdita," whose portrait now hangs in the Wallace Collection. The Duchess of Devonshire and her sister, Lady Duncannon, are well in the centre of the picture; Captain Topham takes in the gay scene through his glass; Doctor Johnson, in a supper box, seems deeply engaged upon his meal, though Mrs. Thrale is on his right and "Bozzy" and Goldsmith are of the party. Captain (later Colonel) Topham, the macaroni, man of taste and editor of The World, appears in another plate of 1785—as "Captain Epilogue," and as "Colonel Topham endeavouring to extinguish the Genius of Holman" (the actor); and to the same date belong "Grog on Board" and "Tea on Shore," as well as the print in colour chosen for illustration to this chapter. "Filial Affection," as this is called, depicting a runaway trip to Gretna Green, speaks so fully for itself that it needs no further description from my pen; but I may mention here its companion print (also published by Mr. Hinton on December 15 of 1785), and called "The Reconciliation, or The Return from Scotland," in which the pair of fugitives—whom we have just seen presenting their horse pistols at the parental poursuivant—have now returned, all penitence and submission, and have won their forgiveness. A very curious and somewhat grisly adaptation of "Filial Affection" is reproduced by Messrs. Bell, to illustrate the article upon Rowlandson in their new and valuable edition of Bryan's Dictionary. It is a plate from The

Dance of Death, an illustrated volume published by Ackermann in 1815, and resembles the earlier print—save that the figure behind the angry parent is a skeleton rider mounted on a skeleton steed. At this point, in touching these two periods (of 1785 and 1815) we may note how far fresher and more spontaneous is the figure-work in that rich period from 1785 onwards. Rowlandson had gained, perhaps, in what we may call his "Dr. Syntax period," in the treatment of landscape perspective or the massing of crowds, but had become more of the caricaturist, had lost the rich organic beauty which really irradiates some of his earlier prints.

A print in colour from my own collection, published by Fores only sixteen days earlier (November 30, 1785) than "Filial Affection," may help here to illustrate my meaning. "Intrusion on Study" or "The Painter Disturbed," shows a very charming model, attired in nothing but the prettiest of mob caps, posing for some goddess on the canvas of the artist, who turns to wave his palette and brushes—a most effective weapon of defence—in the faces of two unwelcome visitors of his own sex, who have just broken in open-mouthed upon his study. The details of the studio, the expressive faces of the artist and his visitors (especially the second), are in Rowlandson's best mood; but what is more interesting, because more exceptional, is the exquisite feeling of line, as subtle as anything Beardsley has recorded, in the girl's recumbent figure—in the flow of the shoulder into the right arm, and in the sweep of the right hip, and faultless drawing of the right hand—which touches a note of purely plastic beauty entirely beyond the reach of either Hogarth or Gillray.

Joseph Grego says of our artist very justly: "Rowlandson's sense of feminine loveliness, of irresistible graces of face expression and attitude, was unequalled in its way; several of his female portraits have been mistaken for sketches by Gainsborough or Morland, and as such, it is possible, since the caricaturist is so little known in this branch, that many continue to pass current."[15] An engraving which came into my own hands, some years ago, of three young girls by Rowlandson, might be an exact illustration of these words, and as the above writer says, be a portrait group by Gainsborough or Hoppner—so refined and yet so masterly was the treatment. I alluded to this print with others, when speaking of Rowlandson as what might be here called a "feminist" in my study of Bartolozzi and his contemporaries, and found illustration there of this peculiarly charming type of his women in "Luxury" (typified, for this artist, by breakfast in bed), "House Breakers," "The Inn Yard on Fire" (where the ladies are making a very impromptu exit), in the lovely model of "The Artist Disturbed," and (for women of fashion) in the series (twelve prints in all) of the "Comforts of Bath."

I mention there, too, that delightful print of "Lady Hamilton at Home," where poor Sir William (whom the caricaturists never neglected) is suffering from an acute attack of gout, while "the lovely Emma, in very classic garb, is watering a flower-pot, and Miss Cornelia Knight, also dressed after the antique, touches the strings of a lyre, and warbles poems of her own composition." In treating, however, of Rowlandson's women, other prints, such as "Tastes Differ," "Opera Boxes," "Harmony," "A Nap in Town," and "In the Country," "Interruption, or Inconvenience of a Lodging House" (published April 1789), and "Damp Sheets" (August 1791), have a strong claim on our notice. Nor must I entirely neglect here Rowlandson's print called "Preparation for the Academy, or Old Joseph Nollekens and his Venus" (1800). It is perhaps the Miss Coleman here upon the model-stand who nearly caused a domestic breach between old Nollekens and his jealous spouse—the group on which he is at work being his "Venus Chiding Cupid," which was modelled for Lord Yarborough. The Life of the Sculptor Nollekens, by his pupil John Thomas Smith, contains some amusing contemporary gossip. He describes the sculptor much as we see him in this plate—his figure short, his head big, his shoulders narrow, his body too large. His worthy better half held strong opinions upon the sculptor's models—"abandoned hussies, with whom she had no patience"; and Miss Coleman having ventured to visit the scene of her early labours in a carriage and pair, the wrath of the virtuous Mrs. Nollekens became unbounded. Words indeed (perhaps a rare defect with the good lady) seem to have failed her at this crisis; in a later interview with Joseph they were not wanting.

But here I would also point out that not only was our caricaturist an unequalled illustrator of lovely woman (and as such makes us often regret that the becoming mob cap has disappeared from use), but also a magnificent landscape artist. I came to notice this especially last year in a very interesting exhibition of Rowlandson's drawings at the Leicester Gallery in London. "A Country Fête," a "Village Scene with Bridge," and the "Promenade on Richmond Hill," were good examples of his delightful handling of English landscape. The last of these formed part of a very interesting set of the artist's original drawings, which were not exhibited, but which I was able to study by kind permission. "Greenwich Park" was among these drawings, with merrymakers racing and tumbling down the hill, and a delicious perspective of the park and hospital; a "Review of Guards in Hyde Park," where, upon the soldiers firing, two of the spectators' horses have bolted into the crowd; the charming drawing in pencil and colour work of two girls called "The Sirens;" rustic scenes such as "Eel Pie Island at Richmond," "Playing Quoits," and a "Rustic Maid Crossing a Stile," to her sweetheart's admiration; such echoes too of war as the crowd cheering the great battleships at Portsmouth, or the print of "Invaders Repulsed," where British troops are seen driving out the French invaders.

Drawn most delicately in pencil with a wash of pure colour, these drawings bring us nearer to the feeling of the artist than even his prints, and it was interesting to compare "Greenwich Hill" in the print and drawing, and to see how much the transcript had lost. Yet seen by themselves the prints were interesting and characteristic. "A Visit to the Uncle" and "to the Aunt," "Travelling in France, 1790"—a signed work showing a large clumsy diligence, which the artist is sketching—"Angelo's Fencing Room," full of contemporary portraits, "The Pleasure of the Country," where fine ladies struggling through the mud find a litter of piglets rushing in among their skirts, were among the best of these, while a print of "Girls Dressing for the Masquerade," and the "Dutch Academy," with a fat model posing before solid Dutchmen, were among those not infrequent prints of our artist whose satire comes near—if not over—the confines of good taste.

Some clever prints of Dr. Syntax himself were here—a subject this which, published by Ackermann under the title of a "Tour of Dr. Syntax in search of the Picturesque" in 1809, was republished in 1812, and occupied the artist in various developments during his later life. To the same period of Rowlandson's career belonged "The Microcosm of London" (1808), "A Mad Dog in a Coffee House" (1809), and "In a Dining Room" (1809), the print called "Exhibition Stare-case, Somerset House" (1811)—where the visitors of both sexes are tumbling headlong downstairs, the extraordinary cleverness of drawing scarcely compensating for the doubtful taste of the subject; and later followed "The World in Miniature" (1816), "Richardson's Show," "The English Dance of Death" (1814-16), and "Dance of Life" (1817), which leads on to the later "Tour of Dr. Syntax in search of Consolation" (1820), and (1821) "In search of a Wife." Although Fores of Piccadilly seems to have published many of our artist's prints during the last years of the eighteenth century, throughout his whole career Rudolph Ackermann remained his constant friend; to the suggestion of this latter was due the idea of a monthly publication, which gave Rowlandson regular employment in his later years, and resulted in the series of prints which I have just detailed, among which the quaint, angular form of Dr. Syntax, with his thin legs, black coat and breeches, and hooked nose, claims a prominent place.

These subjects lead us already into the early nineteenth century, and, as doing so, fall outside our present limit; but Rowlandson himself belongs in his art, as much as Bunbury or Gillray, to the earlier age. An artist of extraordinary genius, we have it on record that two successive Presidents of the Academy in his day, Sir Joshua Reynolds and Sir Benjamin West, in expressing their admiration of his drawings, added their opinion that, had he chosen a higher branch of art, he might have stood in the forefront of English contemporary painting. Instead of this he preferred to devote his genius and his best years to caricature, and in doing so, has bequeathed to us a rich and most precious heritage.

He was happy in his friendships. James Gillray was well known to him; George Morland, that brilliant artist with whom he had so much in common, Henry Angelo, whom he loved to depict among his pupils of the foil ("Angelo's Fencing Room" and "Signora Cigali Fencing at Angelo's"), Bannister, and Ackermann the art publisher were among his intimates. He was less happy in the conduct of his life. Extravagance and carelessness were combined with a passion for gambling which made him a frequent figure in the fashionable playhouses of London; and these habits placed the fortune, which should have been his by industry and inheritance, beyond his reach. The legacy of £7000 bequeathed him by his French aunt, who had treated him so generously in his student days, was speedily dissipated in this way. Indeed, but for the frequent advice and assistance of his friend and publisher, Rudolph Ackermann, he might have found himself in serious difficulties; and the story runs that on one occasion he sat for thirty-six hours at the cards, and that on another, after losing all he had, he sat down coolly to his work and (raising that facile pencil of his) said, "Here is my resource." Thus it was that, after many years of fertile labour, he died a poor man in lodgings at the Adelphi, on the 22nd of April, 1827. His faithful friends of earlier days, Henry Angelo, Bannister, and Rudolph Ackermann, followed to his grave the last great caricaturist of the bygone century.

In these pages we have traced together the record of that century in English Caricature; and if we have been compelled to note but hastily the lesser men, have, in so doing, at least gained breathing space to study four great and typical figures. We saw how William Hogarth, when he handles the graver as humourist and delineator of character, stands forth immortally great; how, when he sought to place himself at the head of the nascent English School, he fell beneath his own level. We saw in Henry William Bunbury the cultured artist, soldier, and man of society, the welcome guest in many a great country-house, who could bring his host's pretty daughters into some charming sketch, or take his part in the improvised theatricals; but whose prints have real humour, charm, and the sweet, wholesome breath of English country life. Then we watched Gillray tower aloft in political satire, and Rowlandson's pencil touch every side of life.

If we noticed at the same time a certain coarseness of fibre come to the surface in much of their work, finding expression often both in subject, and still more in treatment and in type, we must remember that this quality belongs not to the men alone, but to the age. The more sensitive modern may feel himself at first repelled rather than attracted, and many a print of Rowlandson or Gillray find a place in his Index Expurgatorius; but the brutality of these men is the brutality of Nature in some of her moods, and their work, like Nature, fertile, fresh, and vigorous, attracts us (as all strong work will and must) the more we study it by its masterly drawing, its free, open humour, and often its high imaginative grasp.

Behind these men, these Masters of English Caricature, appears, never entirely absent from our thought, the history of the century, with its magnificent record of English achievement. Behind them, too, a corrective and a stimulant to their best effort, is that wonderful revelation of English eighteenth-century pictorial art. For just as when, in years to come, men think on that stirring epoch, the two words England and Liberty will leap unbidden to their thought; so, too, in the record of the greatest epoch of our country's art, a place must be found for the English Caricaturists of the Eighteenth Century.

FOOTNOTES

[1] A fine collection of lithographs of Honoré Daumier (1808-1879) has this year been exhibited in the Victoria and Albert Museum.

[2] "The Works of William Hogarth, elucidated by Descriptions." By T. Clerk. London, 1810.

[3] "William Hogarth," by Austin Dobson; with a valuable technical introduction by Sir W. Armstrong. London, 1902.

[4] "Bartolozzi and his Pupils in England" (Langham Series). By Selwyn Brinton. London, 1903.

[5] "History of Caricature and of Grotesque in Art." By Thomas Wright, M.A., F.S.A. London, 1863.

[6] His "Englishman at Paris" even predates this by four years (1767). The British Museum etchings, to which I allude later, are early work, one even dating from his schooldays at Westminster!

[7] Op. cit. p. 63.

[8] I give a plate of this beautiful Eliza Farren (painted by Lawrence, engraved by Bartolozzi) in my work on Bartolozzi in this Series (facing p. 63). Gillray has an amusing print of the diminutive Lord Derby, standing on his coronet to admire himself in the glass.

[9] They are all enjoying their new diet under similar conditions. In Italy (perhaps the cleverest hit of all) the old Pope, seated, is having the bread shot into his open mouth from a French soldier's blunderbuss, while an assistant at the same moment neatly removes from his head the triple crown.

[10] Mme. Vigée le Brun, in her delightful memoirs, gives some justification to Gillray's severe treatment. Visiting Lady Hamilton soon after Sir William's death she found "this Andromache" draped in black, and extremely fat.

[11] In "Two-penny Whist" appear the worthy Mrs. Humphrey and her maid Betty; in "Push-pin" the Duke of Queensbury and the Duchess of Gordon.

[12] The Magazine of Art, 1901.

[13] Rudolph Ackermann occupies almost the same position to Rowlandson that Mistress Humphrey did to Gillray, as his early and faithful friend and principal publisher.

[14] Bartolozzi and His Pupils in England, p. 46.

[15] Rowlandson, the Caricaturist. By Joseph Grego. 1880.